CONTENTS

GLASTONBURY LAKE VILLAGE

150-50 BCE

DATE FOUND: 1892, BY AN AMATEUR ARCHAEOLOGIST.

Around 2,800 years ago in Britain most tools and weapons were still made from bronze. Then the secrets of making much stronger iron tools and weapons arrived from Europe. A period of history we call the Iron Age began, lasting for about 1,000 years. We find out about life in the Iron Age from remains discovered around Britain. For instance, the remains of a man-made island full of Iron Age huts was discovered near Glastonbury in Somerset.

PLACE FOUND: NEAR GODNEY, SOMERSET.

When amateur archaeologist Arthur Bulleid read about Swiss Iron Age villages built on lakes, he wondered if there were any similar remains around his home in Glastonbury, which had once been a marshy place. Arthur began searching for clues and soon discovered some hummocks in a field. They turned out to be the remains of a man-made island that once stood in water. Excavations unearthed the homes and belongings of people who lived there over 2,000 years ago.

FOUND!

IRON AGE

Moira Butterfield

W
FRANKLIN WATTS

Franklin Watts
First published in Great Britain in 2018 by The Watts Publishing Group

Credits
Series Editor: John C. Miles
Series Designer: Richard Jewitt
Picture Researcher: Diana Morris
Picture Credits: Anteromite/Shutterstock: 1 bg, 2-3 bg, 30-31 bg, 33 bg. Simon Balson/Alamy: front cover main, 21l. Anthony Brown/Dreamstime: 12-13 bg. Colchester Museums: 5l. David Cole/Alamy: 1c, 13tr. Cosma/Shutterstock: back cover br. coxy58/Shutterstock: 15tr. Cranach/Shutterstock: front cover t. c paul fell/Shutterstock: 23tr. Dave G Houser/Getty Images: 17tr. LuFeeTheBear/Shutterstock: front cover bg. National Trust PL/Alamy: 25tr. Jaime Pharr/Shutterstock: 19tr. Photogenès: 18-19 c. Portable Antiquities Scheme/CC Wikimedia: 29tr. Alex Ramsay/Alamy: 29l. Michael Rosskothen/Shutterstock: 5tr. Patrick Rowney/Dreamstime: 24-25 bg. Adam Sorrell/Museum of London: 21tr. Rasiel Suarez/CC Wikimedia Commons: back cover tl. udra11/Shutterstock: front cver bg c. Steve Vidler/Alamy: 16-17. Wessex Archaeology: 7t, 7c, 8-9, 9tr, 11tr, 22-23, 26-27bg, 27tr. WHA/Alamy: 11l, 15l.

HB ISBN 978 1 4451 5302 5
PB ISBN 978 1 4451 5303 2

Printed in China

Franklin Watts
An imprint of
Hachette Children's Group
Part of The Watts Publishing Group
Carmelite House
50 Victoria Embankment
London EC4Y 0DZ

An Hachette UK Company
www.hachette.co.uk

www.franklinwatts.co.uk

This is a reconstruction of a Glastonbury Iron Age island home. Its walls are made of woven sticks and dried mud. Inside there is one dark room, with a hearth in the middle for a fire. There were around 18 homes on the island.

Lots of weaving equipment was left behind, so we know that the islanders wove their own cloth. This is a reconstruction of an Iron Age loom made from branches and stones.

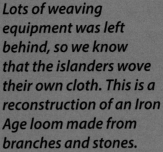

We know from the remains that the island families gathered their food from the surrounding countryside. They ate fish, eels, local birds and even otters and beavers.

The islanders made their own reed baskets, pottery bowls and iron tools such as saws and hammers. To make iron they first heated iron ore (rocks containing iron). Liquid iron ran out and could be cooled, then beaten into different shapes.

The island itself was built from timber, rubble and clay. It stood above the watery marsh, with wooden walkways leading to and from it. A small boat carved from a log was found nearby.

Imagine that you had to do your own weaving, woodworking and metalwork. What do you think you would be good at making?

Iron Age eating
JARLSHOF

Around **200** BCE

During the Iron Age people lived on the southern tip of Shetland, off the coast of north Scotland, in a place we now call Jarlshof. They left behind many clues about how they lived and what they ate, including some of their cooking equipment. The evidence was buried for thousands of years until a storm unearthed it in 1897.

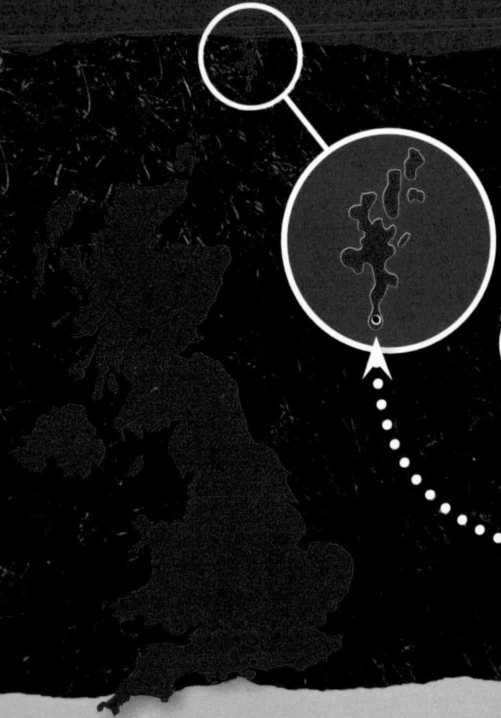

DATE FOUND: 1897, AFTER A STORM. EXCAVATED FROM 1949 ONWARDS.

PLACE FOUND: SUMBURGH HEAD, SHETLAND.

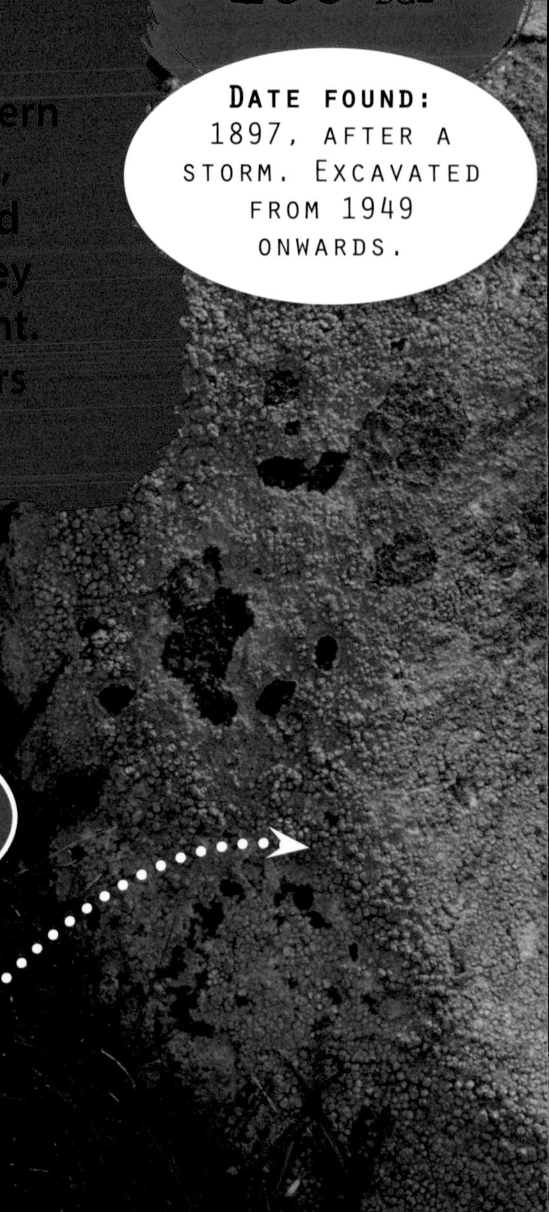

The storm damaged a cliff and revealed the remains of homes from Iron Age times, dating from around 2,200 years ago. The finds showed that Iron Age life involved a lot of hard work. Just to eat daily bread, the people of Jarlshof had to grow crops, harvest grain and grind it to make flour.

This picture shows an Iron Age quern stone from Jarlshof. It was used to grind wheat or barley to make flour. It would have been a hard job for someone crouching on their knees, pushing the small stone over the larger stone to grind up a pile of grain.

Iron Age food mostly consisted of bread, porridge and stews, cooked in pots over a fire and flavoured with wild herbs. We know that the people of Jarlshof also ate shellfish because they left shells behind. You can see them behind this panel.

New inventions such as iron ploughs and sickles made farming crops easier during the Iron Age. Sickles similar to the one shown here were used for cutting crops down.

The people of Jarlshof kept farm animals for meat, milk, cheese and butter. Iron Age butter has actually been found in some parts of Scotland and Ireland, still looking and smelling buttery after 2,000 years! It's called bog butter because it was buried in peat bogs, inside wooden containers. Chemicals in the peat helped preserve the butter.

What foods do you eat that you think Iron Age people would recognise?

A fighting time
DANEBURY HILL FORT

Better farming meant that there was more to eat, so the population of Britain grew during the Iron Age. People began living in large groups we call tribes. Tribes had their own territories and sometimes fought with their neighbours. They began building hilltop bases which we call hill forts. The hill fort of Danebury has revealed gruesome clues about how violent Iron Age life could be.

550 BCE to 50 BCE

DATE FOUND:
1969-1988. REMAINS TURNED UP DURING DECADES OF CAREFUL EXCAVATION.

PLACE FOUND:
STOCKBRIDGE, HAMPSHIRE.

Professor Barry Cunliffe of Southampton University led a team of archaeologists that spent many years excavating Danebury. They discovered the remains of 73 roundhouses, 500 storage buildings and many hundreds of storage pits. The people of Danebury stored their precious supply of grain in the pits and buildings. It's possible that enemies may have attacked them to seize their grain.

The archaeologists found a pit containing the remains of around a hundred bodies, some with sword and spear wounds. This picture shows one of the skulls. It has a spear wound which matches the shape of a typical Iron Age spear, also shown. The remains are a clue that there must have been at least one battle for the fort.

Hill forts such as Danebury were surrounded by ditches, banks and wooden stake fences, making it hard for enemies to get inside. People defending the fort would have used slingshots that looked rather like catapults. They whirled them round to launch stones at their enemies below. They would probably have thrown spears, too. Up close, warriors fought with swords.

Danebury was built on a hill for a good view of the surrounding land. It could be seen from a long way away, impressing local people and helping to warn off enemies.

Tribal chieftains probably lived in hill forts such as Danebury, along with other important tribe members. Members of the tribe farmed the surrounding countryside, but everyone would have rushed into the fort in times of trouble. They would probably have gathered there for important ceremonies, too.

Do you know of any hill forts near where you live? See if you can find one to explore.

A leader's wheels

FERRY FRYSTON CHARIOT BURIAL

Around **500** BCE

DATE FOUND: 2003, DURING NEW ROAD BUILDING.

Most ordinary people weren't buried in Iron Age times, and we don't know what happened to them. But important people were sometimes given burials, along with their belongings. When workmen were building part of a new road in West Yorkshire they found the remains of an important Iron Age man buried in a chariot.

PLACE FOUND: FERRY FRYSTON, WEST YORKSHIRE.

In 2003 a new section of the A1 road was being built in Yorkshire. Archaeologists were on the site in case anything was found during the building work. As they watched the earth-moving machines, the tops of two iron wheels appeared. Just 30 cm below the surface an Iron Age man lay buried in the remains of his chariot! British chariot burials are very rare. They have only ever been found in northern England and are probably a tradition of the Parisi tribe who lived there.

Experts analysing the man's bones got a big surprise when tests showed that he came from either the Highlands of Scotland or Scandinavia, not from Yorkshire. Perhaps he was a great leader of many northern tribes. We can never know for sure.

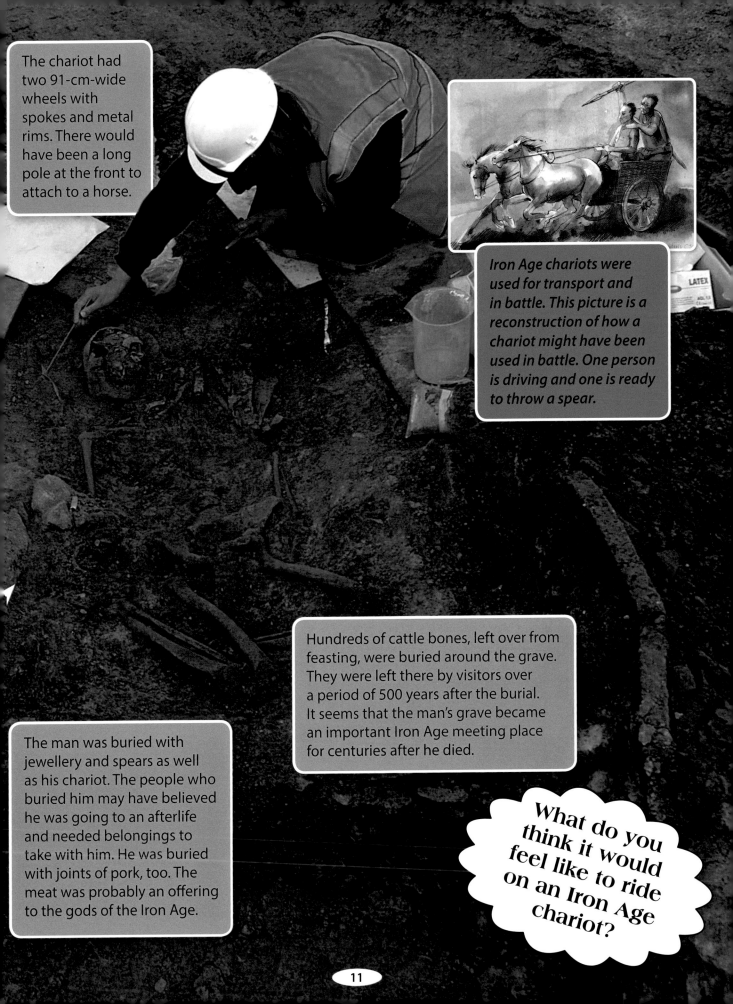

The chariot had two 91-cm-wide wheels with spokes and metal rims. There would have been a long pole at the front to attach to a horse.

Iron Age chariots were used for transport and in battle. This picture is a reconstruction of how a chariot might have been used in battle. One person is driving and one is ready to throw a spear.

Hundreds of cattle bones, left over from feasting, were buried around the grave. They were left there by visitors over a period of 500 years after the burial. It seems that the man's grave became an important Iron Age meeting place for centuries after he died.

The man was buried with jewellery and spears as well as his chariot. The people who buried him may have believed he was going to an afterlife and needed belongings to take with him. He was buried with joints of pork, too. The meat was probably an offering to the gods of the Iron Age.

What do you think it would feel like to ride on an Iron Age chariot?

Magical beings rule

BALLACHULISH GODDESS

Around **600** BCE

DATE FOUND: 1880, BY BUILDERS.

The people of the Iron Age believed in lots of different gods and goddesses. They thought that these magical beings lived in special spots in the countryside such as rivers, springs and woods. That might be why the strange wooden statue of an Iron Age nature goddess was discovered next to a loch in Scotland.

PLACE FOUND: BALLACHULISH, INVERNESS-SHIRE.

Workmen were digging into peat to make the foundations for a wall when they found the nearly life-sized wooden figure of a woman, with white pebbles for eyes. The figure had fallen face-down in the peat, which had kept it damp and well-preserved, along with a screen around it made from woven branches.

Around 2,500 years ago the figure stood on a beach next to Loch Leven, by a dangerous strait where the loch entered the sea. Travellers may have left offerings to the goddess for their safety, but we can't know for sure.

We know a little of Iron Age beliefs from stories that were passed on by word-of-mouth and eventually written down centuries later. One of these old stories tells of a storm goddess called Cailleach, who controlled the wind and storms. Perhaps the wooden figure represents her.

When the Romans arrived in Britain (see page 26) they found that Iron Age Britons had religious leaders called druids. According to the Romans, druids led ceremonies at outdoor shrines, sacrificing animals and even people to their gods and goddesses. Perhaps they led ceremonies by the statue.

This man is dressed the way people imagine druids looked.

Similar carved wooden figures have been found in parts of Britain, Ireland and Europe, often next to rivers and springs. They are sometimes called pole gods. Their left eye is often smaller than their right eye, like the Scottish figure. We don't know why.

What religious statue or picture have you seen?

A mysterious murder
LINDOW MAN

A worker at a Cheshire peat-cutting company got a big shock when a preserved human leg came trundling along his conveyor belt! It turned out to be part of a man who was murdered towards the end of the Iron Age. He is one of several Iron Age murder victims found in peat bogs around northern Europe.

Between
119 BCE
and **2** BCE

DATE FOUND:
1984, UNCOVERED
BY PEAT-CUTTING
MACHINERY.

PLACE FOUND:
LINDOW MOSS,
CHESHIRE.

The peat-cutters called in a local archaeologist who soon uncovered the head and torso of the man's body. The chemicals in the peat had preserved him for 2,000 years, even his skin, hair and nails. Experts began studying him just as they would a murder victim in a modern crime scene. They discovered that he was pushed face-down into the bog after he was killed.

The man had been knocked out and then strangled by a cord that was still tied around his neck. We don't know for sure, but other Iron Age bodies treated in a similar way have been found elsewhere, so it's likely his death was part of a ceremony connected to Iron Age beliefs.

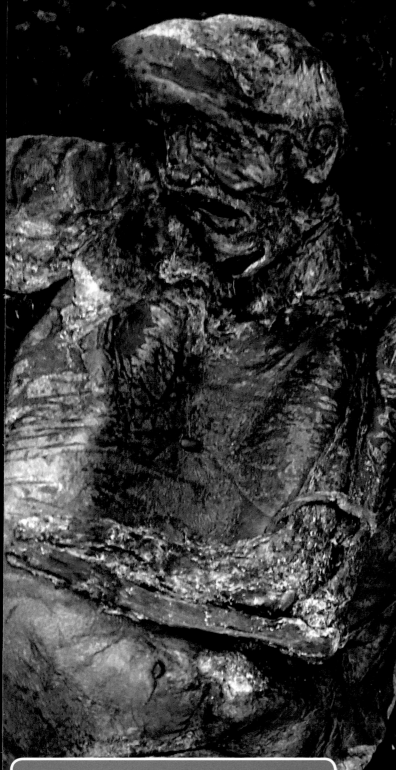

Trying to find facts about the Iron Age is like trying to look for forensic crime evidence. For instance, there was mistletoe pollen in Lindow Man's stomach, a clue that he died in the spring when mistletoe was flowering.

We know that Iron Age people gave offerings to their gods and goddesses to try to please them and ensure good luck. It's possible that the man was a sacrifice made to the gods during hard times, especially as the Romans arrived around the time he died and began conquering Iron Age tribes (see page 26).

Experts were able to reconstruct the man's face from his remains. They found that he had dark hair and a neatly-trimmed beard and moustache. He had neat fingernails, too. If he was used to doing manual work he would probably have had dirty, rough fingernails, so perhaps he was a tribal leader or a druid.

Who do you think the man might have been? Use the clues found by the experts to make a guess.

Swirly art
DESBOROUGH MIRROR

During the Iron Age craftspeople used new skills to decorate the metal objects they made. They added swirly patterns, along with images of animals and human heads. The patterns were put onto valuable objects, including metal mirrors that have been found buried with Iron Age women in Britain. The finest mirror ever found was dug up by accident in Northamptonshire.

Between 50 BCE and CE 50

DATE FOUND: 1908, BY STONE MINERS.

PLACE FOUND: DESBOROUGH, NORTHAMPTONSHIRE.

When local workers were digging for stone they discovered the beautiful Desborough Mirror. The remains of the person who owned it were not found. They were probably cremated (burnt). One side of the bronze mirror was highly polished and the other was decorated. The lucky owner would have been able to look at her reflection in the polished side, instead of just looking in a pond like everybody else!

This swirly patterned art style is called La Tène, after a place in Switzerland where lots of decorated Iron Age objects were found. By the later part of the Iron Age, tribes across Europe were sharing the same art style. They shared ways of living, too. We call them the Celts.

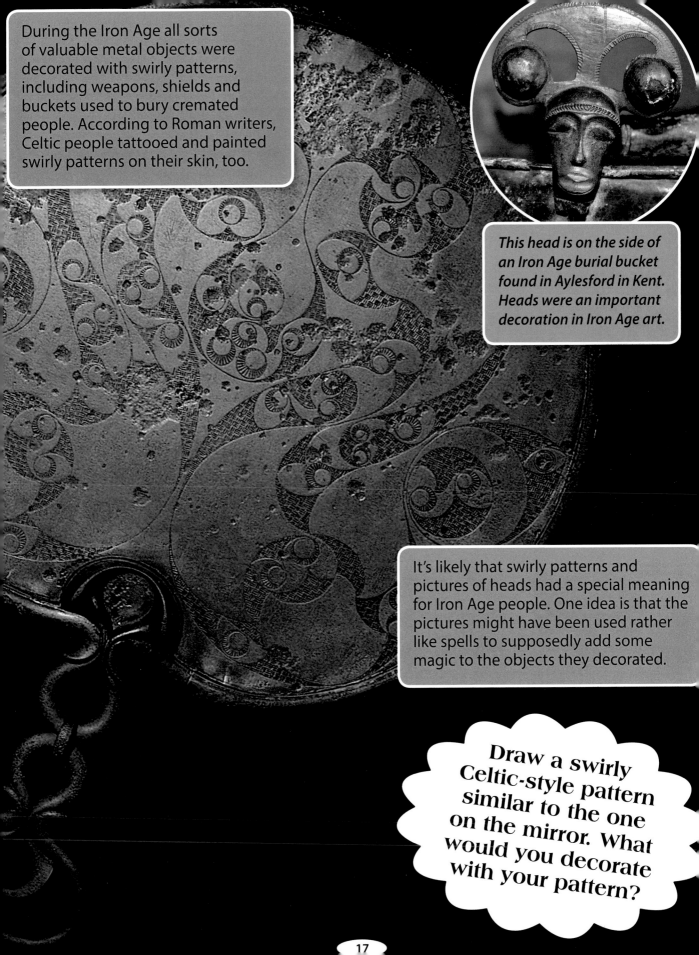

During the Iron Age all sorts of valuable metal objects were decorated with swirly patterns, including weapons, shields and buckets used to bury cremated people. According to Roman writers, Celtic people tattooed and painted swirly patterns on their skin, too.

This head is on the side of an Iron Age burial bucket found in Aylesford in Kent. Heads were an important decoration in Iron Age art.

It's likely that swirly patterns and pictures of heads had a special meaning for Iron Age people. One idea is that the pictures might have been used rather like spells to supposedly add some magic to the objects they decorated.

Draw a swirly Celtic-style pattern similar to the one on the mirror. What would you decorate with your pattern?

water offerings

THE BROIGHTER BOAT

During the Iron Age, many valuable treasures were thrown into rivers and lakes. People may have thought that water was a way into the magical world of their gods and goddesses, and they wanted to please them. One of the finest Iron Age treasures ever discovered was found by the side of Lough Foyle in Northern Ireland. It was a hoard of gold objects, including a tiny golden boat.

Around 100 BCE

DATE FOUND: 1896, BY PLOUGHMEN.

PLACE FOUND: LIMAVADY, NORTHERN IRELAND.

When two Irishmen found a solid lump of metal and mud in the field they were ploughing, they took it home and washed it in a sink. To their amazement, several gold objects appeared. There was a neck ring decorated with magical-looking horses, necklaces, a small bowl shaped like a cauldron and a little golden boat with tiny tools inside.

The boat is 18.4 cm long. It has tiny benches and two rows of nine oars. It even has a paddle rudder, rowlocks for the oars and tiny gold sailor's equipment such as a spear and poles.

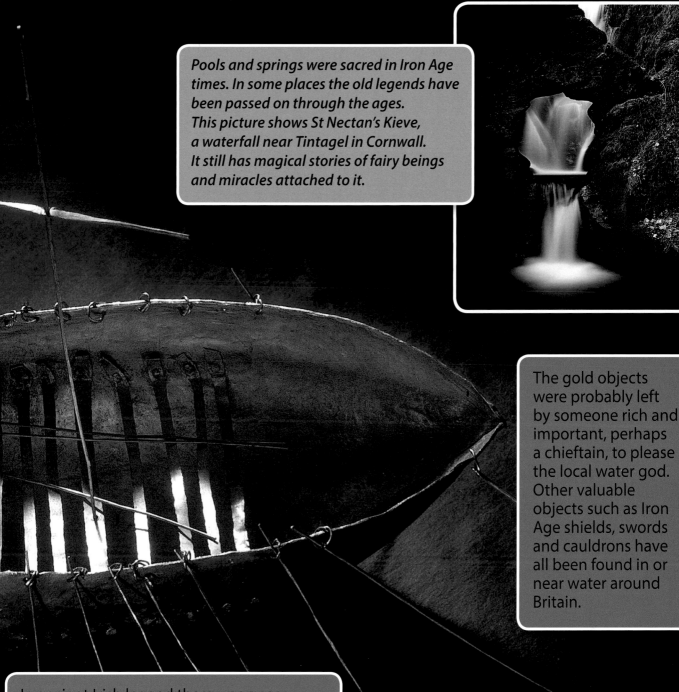

Pools and springs were sacred in Iron Age times. In some places the old legends have been passed on through the ages.
This picture shows St Nectan's Kieve, a waterfall near Tintagel in Cornwall.
It still has magical stories of fairy beings and miracles attached to it.

The gold objects were probably left by someone rich and important, perhaps a chieftain, to please the local water god. Other valuable objects such as Iron Age shields, swords and cauldrons have all been found in or near water around Britain.

In ancient Irish legend there was a sea god called Manannán Mac Lir. He had a magical sailing ship that obeyed thoughts, a cauldron that could bring warriors back to life and a magical horse that could journey over land and sea. The little boat, the mini cauldron and the horse-decorated neck ring may have been offerings for him.

If you were leaving an offering for a magical sea god or goddess, what would you choose to give?

Buried treasure

SNETTISHAM GREAT TORC

Around **75** BCE

DATE FOUND: 1950, BY A PLOUGHMAN.

Towards the end of the Iron Age, tribes around Britain were led by rich powerful chieftains who controlled different areas of the country. The richest leaders and their warriors wore thick gold neck rings called torcs, displaying their wealth and importance to everyone. The finest torc ever found was buried in Norfolk over 2,000 years ago.

PLACE FOUND: SNETTISHAM, NORFOLK.

When a ploughman turned up the Snettisham Great Torc he thought at first that it was a piece of brass bedstead. Luckily he didn't throw it away, because it was actually a heavy Iron Age neck ring made of twisted gold and silver wires. Since it was found, more hidden stashes of Iron Age valuables have been discovered in the same spot, including hundreds more torcs, bracelets, metal bars and coins. Somebody was hiding a lot of treasure there towards the end of the Iron Age!

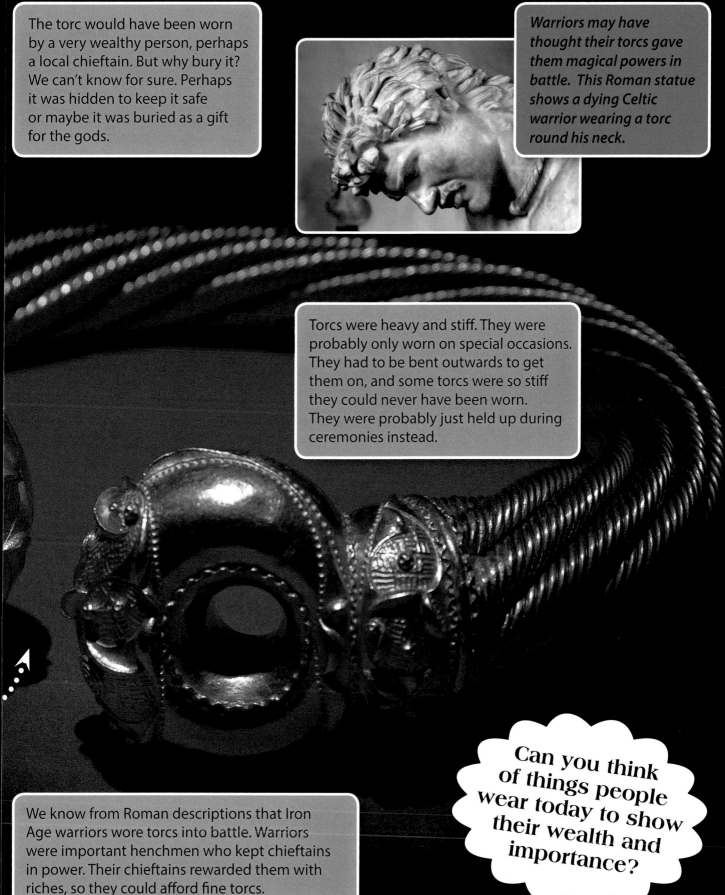

The torc would have been worn by a very wealthy person, perhaps a local chieftain. But why bury it? We can't know for sure. Perhaps it was hidden to keep it safe or maybe it was buried as a gift for the gods.

Warriors may have thought their torcs gave them magical powers in battle. This Roman statue shows a dying Celtic warrior wearing a torc round his neck.

Torcs were heavy and stiff. They were probably only worn on special occasions. They had to be bent outwards to get them on, and some torcs were so stiff they could never have been worn. They were probably just held up during ceremonies instead.

We know from Roman descriptions that Iron Age warriors wore torcs into battle. Warriors were important henchmen who kept chieftains in power. Their chieftains rewarded them with riches, so they could afford fine torcs.

Can you think of things people wear today to show their wealth and importance?

The man with everything
WELWYN GARDEN CITY BURIAL

Towards the end of the Iron Age, Romans ruled
southern Europe. British chieftains became rich
selling goods such as grain and slaves to the Romans.
In return they bought luxury Roman goods.
One of these chieftains was buried in Hertfordshire
with his own Roman wine store.

Around
50-25 BCE

DATE FOUND:
1965, BY GAS MAIN
WORKERS.

PLACE FOUND:
WELWYN GARDEN CITY,
HERTFORDSHIRE.

When workers were cutting a trench for a gas
main in Welwyn Garden City, they discovered
one of the finest Iron Age burials so far found
in Britain. The man who was buried there
had wine jars, a Roman silver cup and all
he needed for a good feast in the afterlife.

The man's body had been
cremated, then wrapped in
the skin of a bear. The bear's
claws were found amongst
the remains. You can see
the pile of cremated bones
above.

Roman wine was stored in tall pottery jars, called amphorae. There were five in the grave, along with feasting plates and cups. Only someone wealthy would have owned so much.

British wheat, wool, metal, slaves and hunting dogs were exported (sold) to Europe. The dogs looked rather like this wolfhound.

We know the names of British Iron Age tribes from Roman records. The Catuvellauni (pronounced cat-oo-vel-orni) tribe ruled in the area where the man was buried. He was probably their chieftain.

Above there is a set of glass pieces that were used in a game rather like the modern game Ludo. The glass used to make the pieces came from as far away as Russia and the Middle East.

Look in your fridge at home. What different countries does the food come from?

The first towns
SILCHESTER

In the later part of the Iron Age the very first towns appeared in Britain. They were founded by Iron Age tribes, and consisted of rows of huts built along rough tracks. The earliest so far discovered belonged to a tribe that may have originally come from France, fleeing from the Romans.

Between
50-30 BCE
The founding of the town

DATE FOUND:
1997, ONWARDS, THE DATE OF MODERN DIGGING.

PLACE FOUND:
SILCHESTER, HAMPSHIRE.

Victorian diggers found Roman treasures in Silchester, but modern archaeologists have dug deeper and uncovered the remains of an Iron Age town called Calleva Atrebatum. It's thought that members of the Atrebates tribe lived here.

This picture shows archaeologists excavating the bones of a puppy buried in Iron Age Silchester. Dogs were carefully buried around the site, along with ravens and even a cat in a jar. The animals may have been offerings to the gods, or perhaps they were buried as some sort of magical protection for the new town.

Silchester may have been founded by a chieftain called Commius. He was the leader of the Atrebates in northern France. At first he was friendly with the Roman ruler Julius Caesar, but then he backed a rebellion that failed. He is believed to have escaped to Britain and settled his people on the site.

Late Iron Age tribes such as the Atrebates began producing coins, some of the earliest ever made in Britain. The coins had pictures of chieftains and tribal symbols on them. This example shows a warrior on a horse.

The Atrebates bought and sold goods around Europe. One of their industries was the making of fur clothing, such as cloaks. Lots of tiny bones have been found, a clue that the cloaks were probably made from puppy fur.

The Iron Age people of Calleva Atrebatum had sophisticated tastes. They ate from plates (very modern in Iron Age times) and they flavoured their food with coriander, fennel and poppy seeds, in the Roman way. They also ate olives. The earliest olive ever found in Britain turned up at the dig.

If you were to design a coin for the area where you live, what pictures would you put on it?

Conquered!
MAIDEN CASTLE

Around 2,000 years ago, in CE 43, the Roman army arrived to conquer Britain. They landed on the south coast and then pushed north and west. We know that some tribes tried to fight back, but could a skeleton discovered at Maiden Castle in Dorset provide a clue to what happened? It's not easy to get answers from so long ago!

CE 43
Roman invasion date

DATE FOUND:
BETWEEN 1934-37.
THE DATES OF THE
EXCAVATION.

PLACE FOUND:
MAIDEN CASTLE,
DORSET.

A famous archaeologist called Sir Mortimer Wheeler excavated the Iron Age hill fort of Maiden Castle. He found lots of human remains with violent wounds, including the skeleton of a man with a spearhead stuck in his spine. We know that the Romans fought a tribe called the Durotriges at the fort. Sir Mortimer Wheeler claimed that the bodies dated from the battle, but some archaeologists disagreed with him. We do know one thing for sure. The Iron Age was a very violent time!

The skeleton at the front has a spearhead in its spine. The spear might not have killed the man, but the blow to his head would have done. His skull has a big hole in it.

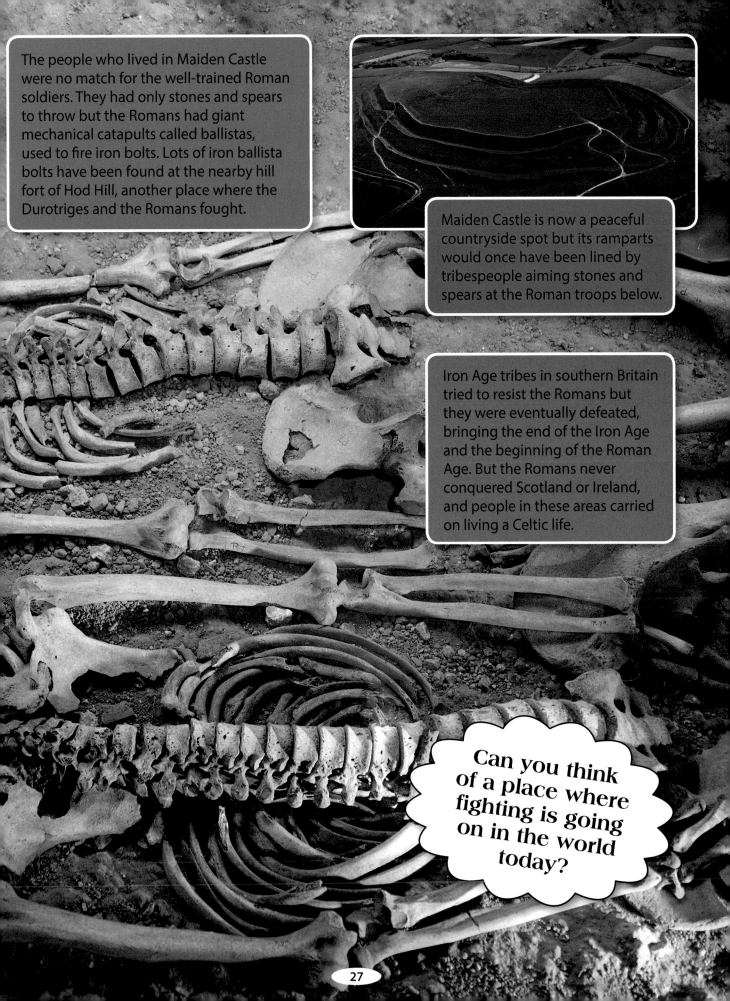

The people who lived in Maiden Castle were no match for the well-trained Roman soldiers. They had only stones and spears to throw but the Romans had giant mechanical catapults called ballistas, used to fire iron bolts. Lots of iron ballista bolts have been found at the nearby hill fort of Hod Hill, another place where the Durotriges and the Romans fought.

Maiden Castle is now a peaceful countryside spot but its ramparts would once have been lined by tribespeople aiming stones and spears at the Roman troops below.

Iron Age tribes in southern Britain tried to resist the Romans but they were eventually defeated, bringing the end of the Iron Age and the beginning of the Roman Age. But the Romans never conquered Scotland or Ireland, and people in these areas carried on living a Celtic life.

Can you think of a place where fighting is going on in the world today?

All change
FISHBOURNE PALACE

CE 65

onwards

DATE FOUND:
1960, BY A LOCAL
FARMER.

Some southern British tribal leaders worked with the Romans, helping them to govern. In return they were rewarded with riches and power. One of these leaders may have had a fine Roman-style palace near Chichester, living in a way that was very different from earlier times.

PLACE FOUND:
FISHBOURNE,
WEST SUSSEX.

A local Chichester farmer was digging a trench for a water main when he uncovered mosaic floors that had not been glimpsed for many centuries. Archaeologists excavated the site and discovered the remains of a palace built during the first years of Roman rule in southern Britain. It might have belonged to a local tribal chieftain who now lived in Roman-style luxury.

The palace had expensive mosaic floors such as the one in the picture. It shows the Roman god Cupid riding a dolphin. The owner obviously wanted Roman pictures, not British ones! He probably employed craftsmen from abroad to create his new floors.

The owner may have been a local chief called Cogidubnus. He was the leader of the Regni tribe, but he became a client ruler, which meant he worked closely with the Romans. He became Romano-British – living in a Roman, not a Celtic, way.

This reconstruction of a room at Fishbourne Palace shows Roman-style furniture and decorations, a far cry from the huts of Iron Age British tribes.

Though Iron Age life came to an end in southern Britain with the Roman invasion, some tribal leaders did not go quietly. In CE 60 or 61 some Celtic tribes, led by Queen Boudica, rebelled against the Romans. They attacked and destroyed the Roman towns of Colchester, St Albans and London, killing up to 80,000 people before eventually being defeated in battle.

Fishbourne Palace had around a hundred rooms, the latest underfloor heating and a Roman-style garden with fountains and elegant statues.

Would you choose to live in Iron Age or Roman times? Why?

Glossary

Amateur Someone who does something for fun, rather than as a job

Afterlife The belief that someone who dies will go on to lead another life.

Amphorae Pottery wine containers imported into Britain from the Roman Empire.

Ballista A giant mechanical catapult used by the Roman army for firing iron bolts. This weapon was used against Iron Age tribes in southern Britain.

Bog butter A wooden container of Iron Age butter buried in a peat bog to keep it fresh.

Celtic The name given to all the people who lived across northern Europe during the Iron Age. They shared similar beliefs and ways of life.

Cremated When a body is burnt, rather than buried.

Druids Priests who carried out religious ceremonies and gave advice to chieftains during Iron Age times. Druids were pagan, which meant they believed in many gods and goddesses, not the one god of the Bible.

Hill fort An Iron Age settlement on top of a hill, surrounded by defensive ditches and earth banks.

Iron Age A period of history which, in southern Britain, was roughly between 800 BCE and CE 43.

Iron ore Rocks containing iron. When heated, the liquid iron runs out.

La Tène The name given to the swirly art style that was used in later Iron Age times.

Loom A piece of equipment used to weave cloth from thread.

Peat A type of soil made from rotten plants, found in boggy places. The chemicals in peat help to preserve some materials.

Pole gods The name we give to Iron Age wooden figures that represented gods and goddesses.

Preserved Kept from rotting away.

Quern stone A stone used to grind up grain to make flour.

Ritual A ceremony done in the same way every time.

Romano-British British people who lived under Roman rule and took on the Roman way of life after the end of the Iron Age.

Romans People who came from a civilisation based in Rome. They eventually conquered southern Britain.

Sacrifice A killing made to please a god. Iron Age people sacrificed animals and may also have sacrificed people.

Shrine A special location for a religious ceremony.

Sickle A farm tool for cutting down crops by hand.

Slingshot An Iron Age weapon similar to a catapult, for firing stones.

Torc A Celtic neck ring made from twisted wires.

Further Information

WEBLINKS

www.bbc.co.uk/wales/celts/

Explore a bog to turn up Iron Age treasure.

www.ancientcraft.co.uk/Archaeology/iron-age/ironage_food.html

Learn about Iron Age food and try a recipe.

ironage-history.com/brigantia/kit_clothing.htm

Some tips on making your own Iron Age-style torc and clothing.

Note to parents and teachers: Every effort has been made by the Publishers to ensure that the websites in this book are suitable for children, that they are of the highest educational value, and that they contain no inappropriate or offensive material. However, because of the nature of the Internet, it is impossible to guarantee that the contents of these sites will not be altered. We strongly advise that Internet access is supervised by a responsible adult.

TIMELINE

800 BCE   The secret of making iron began to spread across Britain from Europe. The period we call the Iron Age began, replacing the time we call the Bronze Age.

700 BCE   The first hill forts began to appear in Britain.

500–100 BCE   The biggest hill forts we know of were built.

500 BCE   The Ferry Fryston chariot burial was among a number of chariot burials in northern England around this time.

300 BCE   Iron Age craftspeople began to decorate iron objects with swirling patterns.

100 BCE   Coins were used for the first time in Iron Age Britain.

50 BCE   Roman troops arrived for the first time on British shores. They didn't stay, but they made some British allies.

50 BCE   The Atrebates tribe were living in Silchester, one of Britain's first towns.

2 BCE   Lindow Man was sacrificed in a peat bog in Cheshire.

CE 43   The Roman army began to conquer southern Britain and Wales, but did not conquer Ireland or Scotland.

CE 65   The building of Fishbourne Palace was begun. People in southern Britain began to live in a more Roman way.

Index